Easy Tatting

Rozella F. Linden

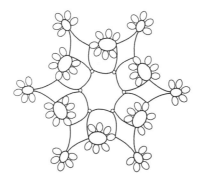

DOVER PUBLICATIONS, INC.
Mineola, New York

Bibliographical Note

Easy Tatting is a new work, first published by Dover Publications, Inc., in 1999.

International Standard Book Number: 0-486-29986-4

Manufactured in the United States of America
Dover Publications, Inc., 31 East 2nd Street, Mineola, N.Y. 11501

Introduction

The origin of tatting is somewhat of a mystery. However, it was all the rage in the 18th and 19th century among well-to-do and fashionable ladies—"fine work for fine ladies." The term "picot" is French and many credit French aristocrats with inventing tatting. Perhaps it was borrowed from the working class, who used a similar technique to mend their fishing nets. After fine lace became available in stores, the art of making homemade lace declined for several decades. Today the interest in tatting is growing and many people want to revive the "lost art" of making tatted lace.

The first 90% of learning to tat is learning to make the knot or double stitch. The other 90% is figuring out the instructions. This is reality, not math.

Tatting instructions can be very cryptic. Often those who know how to tat still have trouble with the instructions in most tatting pattern books. I often have to try two or three times before I get some patterns to come out right! The purpose of this book is to provide tatting instructions and patterns for beginners and anyone else who would benefit from *seeing* "how to do it."

The illustrations were done using a CAD program and are not always exactly to scale. I have, however, attempted to draw them as close as possible to the correct proportions.

Numbers are used to indicate how many double stitches there are in a ring or chain, or between picots.

Letters in the illustrations refer to the written instructions and are used to show where to begin, where to join, etc.

Equipment Needed for Tatting

Tatting shuttle: A metal one with a removable bobbin and a hook on one end for joining is recommended. Keep extra bobbins on hand for use with different colors of thread. All the projects in this book use one tatting shuttle.

Thread: Beginners should use a thick crochet thread—size 5, 8, or 10 will do. It is easier to learn to tat using a variegated color thread, because the double stitch is easier to see on contrasting colors. *Pearl cotton* feels, and looks, great and is pleasant to work with. Some crochet thread is not suitable for tatting because it does not have a tight enough twist. *Tatting thread* (size 70) is very fine. A proficient tatter can quickly make beautiful delicate lace with this kind of thread. The Snowflake Ornament (*page 20*) is made with fine tatting thread.

Crochet hook, or large sewing needle: This is used to work in the ends.

Scissors or other cutting instrument: A pair of nail clippers fit easily in a tatting bag with the other equipment. Small scissors or a seam ripper will also work well.

Quilter's T-pins: These are used for positioning and blocking the finished piece.

Stiffening medium: My grandmother always used sugar water to stiffen her "fine things." Corn starch, laundry starch, or commercial stiffening products made especially for crocheted and tatted items also work. Spray starch tends to flake off and look nasty, and is not recommended.

Small zippered bag: All the essentials fit easily in a "to go" tatting bag. The time spent waiting for an appointment can be profitably spent working on a tatting project. This is a good way to meet people, as I am often interrupted by someone inquiring about what I'm making.

Abbreviations

+	picot used for joining
=	join to picot already made
–	small picot
– –	medium picot
– – –	large picot
– – – –	very large picot
ds	double stitch

Ring (3 = 3 – 3 – – 2 – – – 1 – – – – 1 – – – 2 – – 3 – 3 + 3)

Work a ring with 3 double stitches, join to previous ring, work 3 double stitches, small picot, 3 double stitches, medium picot, 2 double stitches, large picot, 1 double stitch, very large picot, 1 double stitch, large picot, 2 double stitches, medium picot, 3 double stitches, small picot, 3 double stitches, small picot to be used for joining another ring later, 3 double stitches. Close ring.

Chain (6 – 6)
A chain of 6 double stitches, small picot, 6 double stitches.

Turn
This means to turn the work over. Sometimes called "reverse work" (RW) in tatting instructions.

Basic Tatting Instructions

First half of double stitch
Hold thread as shown (*Fig. 1*).

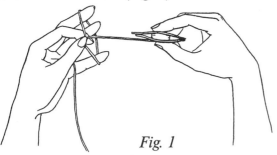

Fig. 1

Work the double stitch between the first finger and the middle finger. The thread around the right hand forms a loop. Pass the shuttle *under* the thread in the left hand, then back *over* (*Fig. 2*).

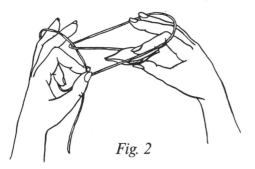

Fig. 2

At this point the knot is around the thread in the left hand. Relax the left hand so that the thread is limp. Transfer the knot to the shuttle thread by pulling the shuttle thread tight, then spreading the fingers of the left hand to pull the knot into place (*Fig. 3*).

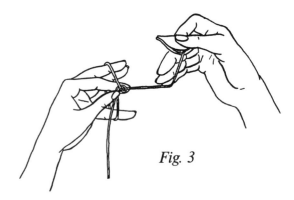

Fig. 3

Second half of double stitch
The thread between the shuttle and the left hand hangs in a loop. Pass the shuttle *over* the thread in the left hand, then back *under* it (*Fig. 4*).

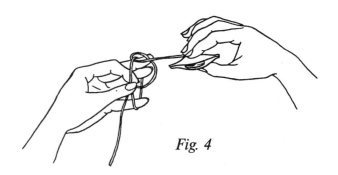

Fig. 4

Transfer the knot as before *(Fig. 5)*.

A correct double stitch will easily slide back and forth on the shuttle thread. To close a ring, slide all the double stitches together by pulling the shuttle thread while holding the double stitches with the left hand.

A space left between two double stitches makes a *picot* (pronounced *peek-oh*), when the knots slide together by closing a ring or pulling a chain together *(Fig. 6)*.

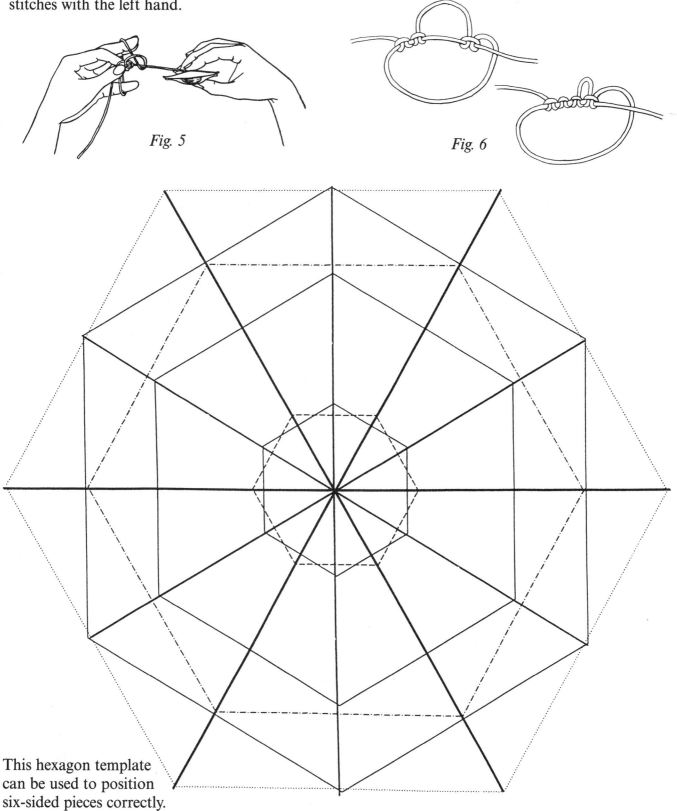

Fig. 5

Fig. 6

This hexagon template can be used to position six-sided pieces correctly.

5

Part One—Just Rings

One tatting shuttle filled with any size and color thread will make all these items.
Size 8 white crochet cotton was used for the examples in this book.
Many of these items are used as part of the more involved projects later.

Center Ring 1A

Ring (4 – 4 – 4 – 4 – 4 – 4) Close ring and tie ends to make sixth picot. This is used when a row of chains is worked around the center ring. See the Small Snowflakes and Flowers (*page 14*).

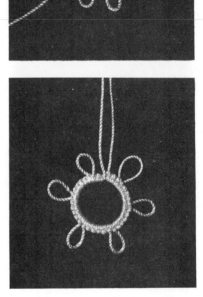

Center Ring 1B

Ring (2 – 4 – 4 – 4 – 4 – 4 – 2) Close ring and work in ends. This is used in many of the later projects.

Center Ring 1A   Center Ring 1B

Fancy Flower
Six rings are joined together in a circle.

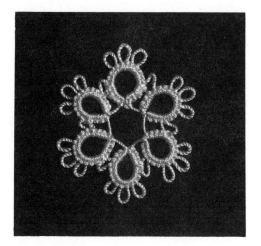

First ring (3 + 3 – 2 – 2 – 3 + 3) Close ring. The first and last picots join the ring to the rings beside it. The remaining three picots are just for decoration and can be made all the same size or small, medium, small for a scallop effect.
Leave a 1/8" space on the thread.

Next ring (3 = 3 – 2 – 2 – 3 + 3) Join this ring to the last picot of the previous ring. To do this, work the first 3 ds. Hold the work so that the picot is on top of the thread around your left hand. Using the hook or point on the end of your shuttle, or a crochet hook, draw this thread through the picot to form a loop (*Fig. 1*). Insert the shuttle, through this loop from right to left. Pull gently on the thread around your left hand to draw up the loop close to the previous stitch. This counts as the first half of a double stitch. Work the second half of the double stitch. Complete the ring as before.
Leave a space on the thread.
Work in this way until there are five rings.

Last ring (3 = 3 – 2 – 2 – 3 = 3) Join to the *first* picot made on the *first* ring. To do this, you must bring this picot into the proper position. Fold the previous rings up so that the back is facing you, and the first picot is next to the loop of thread around your left hand. Insert the hook or point of the shuttle, or a crochet hook, through the picot from back to front, then twist it. Draw up a loop of thread and pass the shuttle through as before (*Fig. 2*); complete the double stitch and the ring. Cut the thread and tie the ends together at the base of the first ring; work in the ends.

Fig. 1. Joining picots.

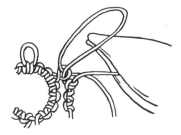

Fig. 2. Joining the last ring to the first ring.

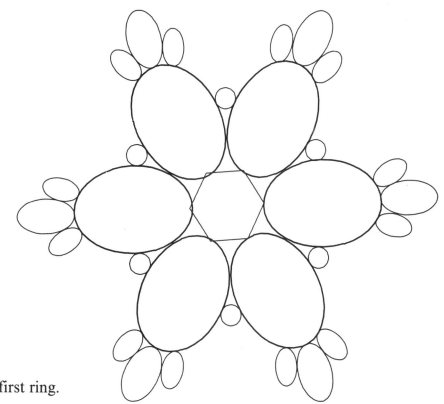

Tatted Earrings

Use any color beads and thread. The beads should have a hole large enough for two strands of thread to fit through.

String six beads on the shuttle thread. Five of them must be on the thread wound around the left hand to make the ring. The picots are just the size of the beads, which are slid into place one at a time with two double stitches between them.

The sixth bead will be slid into place after the ring is closed.

Leave a tail of about 6" of thread before making the ring.

Ring (2, bead, 2, bead, 2, bead, 2, bead, 2, bead, 2) Close ring and cut thread leaving about 6" attached to ring.

Use a needle or crochet hook to pull the tail through the sixth bead and slide this bead all the way down to the ring. Tie a knot in both threads to hold this bead in place, or use a tiny dab of hot glue. Fasten through an earring wire and tie another knot in both threads about ¾" to 2" away from ring. Trim off the excess thread.

Make another earring exactly the same as the first.

The length can be measured by inserting a quilter's T-pin through the ring into a piece of heavy cardboard, and another at the desired length. The knot which determines the length is tied around the second T-pin. Remove the pins after the knot is tightened. For the second earring insert the T-pins back into the holes made for the first earring.

Star Suncatcher

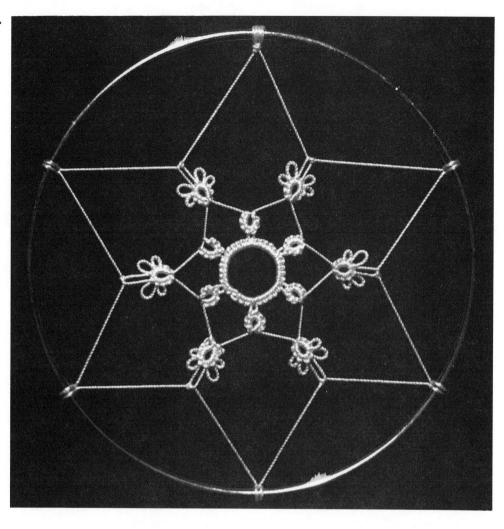

Begin with center ring like 1B (*page 6*) made with very small picots.

Ring (3 + 6 + 6 + 6 + 6 + 6 + 3) Close ring, work in ends.

Outside row
  Small ring (3 = 3) This is joined to the center ring.
  Turn and leave about ½" space.
  Large ring (4 – 1 –– 1 ––– 1 –– 1 – 4) Close ring. The five picots are for decoration. Make them small, medium, large, medium, small.
  Turn and leave about ½" space
  Repeat from small ring around so there are six small and six large rings. Tie at the base of one of the large rings and work in the ends.

Center in a 5" brass ring using T-pins and stretch in place with a piece of thread worked around through each large picot and around the brass ring.

The hexagon template on page 5 may be used to position the star correctly. A bit of hot glue may be used to keep the thread in place on the brass ring.

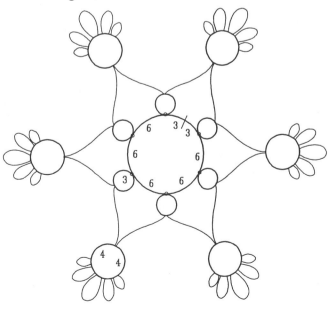

Ice Crystal

This is similar to the star suncatcher, but has many very large picots that are rolled back and forth several times between the thumb and first finger to make them icy looking.

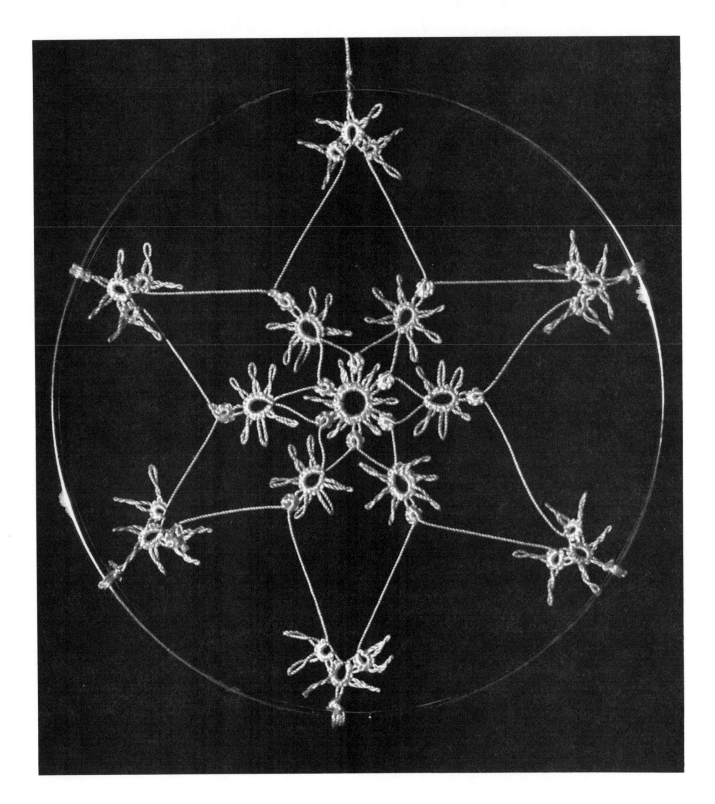

Center ring (1 + 2 − − − − 2 + 2 − − − − 2 + 2 − − − −2 + 2 − − − −2 + 2 − − − −2 + 2 − − − −1) Close ring, work in ends. There are six very small picots to which the next row is joined, alternating with six very large picots for decoration.

First row

Small ring (3 = 3) Join to center ring. Close ring.

Turn and leave ½" space.

Large ring (2 − − − −2 − − − −2 − − − −2 + 2 − − − −2 − − − −2 − − − −2) There are six large picots for decoration and a small picot in the center. The second row is joined to this row by the center picots of these rings.

Turn and leave ½" space.

Repeat around so there are six rings. Tie ends and work in at base of large ring.

Second row

Small ring (3 = 3) Join to last row.

Turn and leave about 1" to 1½" space.

Clover of three rings:

Ring one (2 − − − − 2 − − − − 2 + 2) Close ring.

Ring two (2 = 2 − − − − 2 − − − − 2 − − − − 2 + 2) Close ring.

Ring three (2 = 2 − − − − 2 − − − − 2) Close ring.

Turn and leave about 1" to 1½" space.

Repeat around so there are six small rings and six clovers. Tie ends and work in at base of clover.

Detail

Part Two—Easy Chains

One shuttle and a second thread from a ball of thread are used for all of these items. If the ring thread and chain thread are to be the same color, fill the shuttle and leave it attached to the ball.

A second ball of the same thread makes it possible to fill the shuttle again and just continue using the first ball for the chain thread. Fewer knots and ends to be worked in make the piece look better when it is finished—and also require less work.

Chain

To make a chain, wrap the ball thread around the little finger of the left hand as shown (*Fig. 1*). Work the double stitches the same as for the rings.

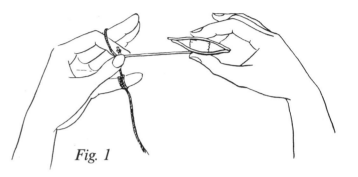

Fig. 1

Lock join

Lock joins are used to join chains to picots that are below and to the right of the chain. They do not slide on the thread. To make a lock join, pull a loop of *shuttle* thread through the joining picot (*Fig. 2*). Pass the shuttle through this loop, carefully ease the join into position and tighten the thread.

Fig. 2

Flower with One Picot
In the Center

Ring one (6 + 3 – – – – 3 + 6) Close ring.
Turn
Chain (6 – 1 – –1 – 6)
Turn
Repeat chains and rings around until there are six rings and six chains, joining rings as follows:

Rings two through five (6 = 3 = 3 + 6) Join first picot to previous ring and second picot to large center picot of the first ring. Close ring.
Ring six (6 = 3 = 3 = 6) Join this ring to the fifth ring, the center picot of the first ring and to the free picot of the first ring made. Close ring.

Each ring is joined to the ones beside it and to the very large center picot of the first ring. Join the last chain to the base of the first ring; tie the threads and work in the ends.

Small Rosette

This is the center of the Eight-Inch Doily in Part Three. There are twelve rings, each joined to the rings beside it.

Ring one (3 + 3 – 3 + 3) Close ring.
Turn
Small chain (3 – 3)
Turn
Ring
Turn
Large chain (7 – 7)
Turn
Ring
Repeat rings and chains, alternating large and small chains around, working rings as follows:

Rings two through eleven (3 = 3 – 3 + 3) Join to previous ring.

Ring twelve (3 + 3 – 3 = 3) Join to previous ring and to first ring made.
Tie threads at beginning and work in ends.

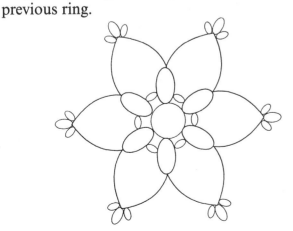

Flower with One Picot in the Center

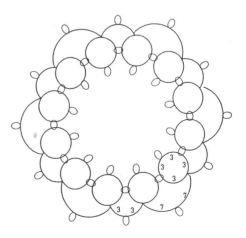

Small Rosette

Small Snowflakes and Flowers

For flowers, use a different color thread for the center ring than that used in the row of chains worked around the center. If done in white they look like snowflakes.

A center ring with larger picots is very different from one with small picots. Either may be used, depending on the look desired.

Start with a center ring like 1A (*page 6*)

Ring (3 + 3 + 3 + 3 + 3 + 3) Close ring and tie ends to form sixth picot. Do not cut the thread if you are planning to continue with the same color.

Turn

Outside row of chains

    Chain (6 – 1 – – 1 – 6)

    Lock join to next picot of center ring.

    Repeat chains around, joining to all the center ring picots. Tie ends at the beginning of the outside row and work in the ends.

Large Rosette

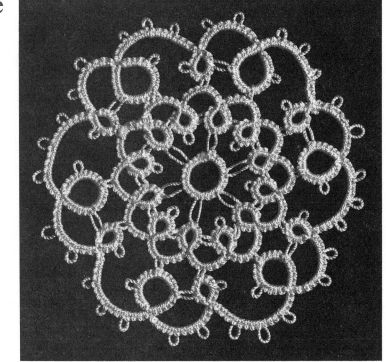

Begin with center ring like 1B (*page 6*) made with large picots.

Ring (2 + 4 + 4 + 4 + 4 + 4 = 2) Close ring, work in ends.

Row of rings and chains There are 12 rings.

  Ring (3 + 3 = 3 + 3) First picot is joined to previous ring (except on first ring); middle picot is joined to the center.

  Turn

  Chain (4 + 4)

  Turn

  Ring (3 = 3 – 3 + 3) Join to previous ring; do *not* join to center.

  Repeat rings and chains around, joining each ring to previous ring. Join last ring to first ring made.

Outside row of rings and chains (Sweet & sour rings)

  Small ring (3 – 3 = 3 + 3) Join to chain picot of previous row.

  Turn

  Small chain (4 – 4 – 4)

  Turn

  Large ring (6 = 6 = 6 – 6) Join to previous ring and to next chain of last row.

Turn

Large chain (4 – 4 – 4 – 4)

Repeat around, joining all rings to the previous row of chains, and each pair of large and small rings together. There are six pairs of rings.

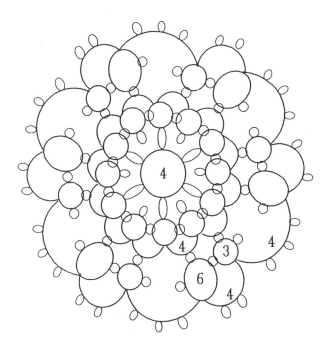

15

Small Heart Edging
or Insertion

Heart

   Ring (1 –– 1 –– 1 –– 1 ––– 1 –– 1 ––– 1 –– 1 –– 1 –– 1)

   Turn

   Chain (2 + 3 – 1 –– [total of 17 medium picots each separated by 1 DS]

   Lock join at A

   Chain 1 –– 1 –– 1 ––– 1 – – – – 1 ––– 1 –– 1 ––)

   Lock join at B.

   Chain (1 –– [total of 17 medium picots each separated by 1 ds] 1 – 3 = 2) Join at C.

   Tie ends at base of ring, work in ends to finish.

   Make desired number of hearts.

Top border

   Work **turn**, **chain** (3 – 3), **turn**, between all rings.

   Ring one (3 – 6 + 3) This is the ring between hearts.

   Ring two (3 = 3 = 3 + 3) Join to ring one and then to the fourth picot from the top center (D) of a small heart.

   Ring three (3 = 6 + 3)

   Ring four (3 = 3 = 3 + 3) Join to ring three and then to the fourth picot from the other top center (E) of the same small heart.

   Repeat, joining next ring one to previous ring four (see diagram).

Bottom border

   Work **turn**, **chain** (3 – 3), **turn**, between all rings

   Ring one (3 – 3 – 3 + 3) This is the ring between hearts.

   Ring two (3 = 6 + 3) Join to ring one.

   Ring three (3 = 3 = 3 + 3) Join to ring two and then to the very large picot of the bottom center ring of a small heart (F).

   Ring four (3 = 6 + 3) Join to ring three.

   Repeat, joining next ring one to previous ring four as in illustrations.

Large Heart

Ring one (1 – – 1 – – 1 – – 1 – – 1 – – – 1 – – 1 – – 1)

Turn

Chain 6

Turn

Ring two (1 – – 1 – – 1 – – – 1 – – 1 – – – 1 – – 1 – – 1)

Turn

Chain 6

Turn

Ring three (1 – – 1 – – 1 – – – 1 – – 1 – – 1 – – 1 – – 1)

Turn

Chain (6 + 3 – 2 – – [total of 10 picots with 2 ds between each of them]

Lock join at A

Chain (1 – – [total of 5 picots with 2 ds between each of them]

Lock join at B

Chain (1 – – 2 – – 2 – – 2 – – – 2 – – – – 2 – – – 2 – – 2 – – 2 – – 2)

Lock join at C

Chain (1 – – [total of 5 picots with 2 ds between each of them]

Lock join at D

Chain (1 – – [10 picots with 2 ds between each of them] 1 – 3 = 6) Join to first small picot of chain.

Tie ends at beginning of first ring.

The heart-shaped outline of this piece is due to the consistent size of the chain picots, with the top picots smaller and the picots at the bottom point larger. This is excellent practice making picots!

Five-Inch Snowflake

Center ring 1B made with large picots.
   Ring (2 – – –4 – – – 4 – – –4 – – –4 – – –4 – – –2)

Outside row
   Small ring (3 = 3) Join to center.
   Turn
   Chain 10
   Ring (3 – – – –3)
   Turn
   Chain (5 – – 1 – – 1 – – 5)
   Turn
   Ring (3 = 3) Join to very large picot of previous ring.
   Turn
   Chain (10 – – 1 – – 1 – – 10)
   Turn
   Ring (3 = 3) Join to the same very large picot as before.
   Turn
   Chain (5 – – 1 – – 1 – – 5)
   Turn
   Ring (3 = 3) Join to the same very large picot.
   Turn
   Chain 10
   Turn
   Repeat around.
   Tie ends at beginning and work in.

18

Tatted Flower Pin

Center
Ring (2 – – 4 – – 4 – – 4 – – 4 – – 4 – – 2)

Beads and chains

Using a small crochet hook, slide a bead onto one of the picots of the center ring. Put the crochet hook through the hole in the bead and pick up the thread of the picot, pulling it through the hole. With the picot still on the hook, pick up the shuttle thread and pull it through the picot until it makes a loop large enough to pass the shuttle through. This is just a lock join the same as in the small snowflake, except that there is a bead on the picot. The chain will hold the bead in place.

Chain (3 – 1 – – 1 – – 1 – – – 1 – – – 1 – – 1 – – 1 – 3) Slide a bead onto the next picot of the center ring and lock join to this picot.

Repeat around so that all six picots of the center ring have a bead and the row of chains is joined to each one. Tie the ends around the chain at the first bead so that the row of chains ends where it begins. Work in the ends.

A small pin or pierced earring may be inserted into the hole of the center ring and used to fasten it to a shirt or jacket. Or, the pin may be glued to a jewelry pin or sewed onto a garment.

Variations: Make five picots in the center ring. Add more picots to the row of chains for larger petals, or join the petals together with a picot, adding three more double stitches to the beginning and end of each chain.

Optional picot (not in written instructions)

Snowflake Ornament

Large ring (1 – – 1 – – 1 – – 1 – – 1 – – 1 – – 1 – – 1) Seven picots.
Turn
Chain (6 + 6 + 6)
Lock join to middle picot of large ring just made.
Chain 6
Turn

Small ring (1 – – 1 – – 1 – – 1 – – 1 – – 1) Five picots.
Turn
Chain 6
Repeat until there are six sides, six points, six large, and six small rings. The chain is joined at picot A. Attach the snowflake to a small brass ring.

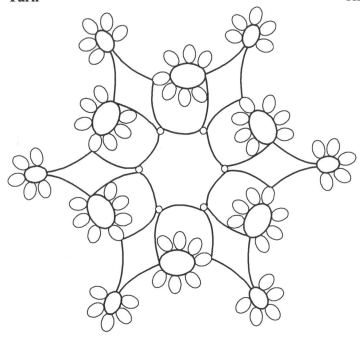

Snowflake

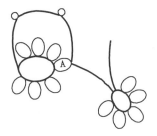

Detail of snowflake

Lacy Square

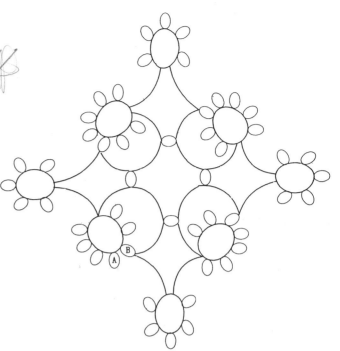

Work as for snowflake, joining the chain at picot B (see diagram). There are four large and small rings in the square.

Circle-in-a-Square

Ring (2 + 4 + 2)
Turn
Large chain (4 – 1 – 4)
Turn
Ring (2 = 4 + 2) All eight rings join together in a circle.
Turn
Small chain (3 – 3)
Repeat until there are eight rings and four large and four small chains.
Tie ends and work in.

Part Three—Elegant Projects

Fancy Snowflake

This design is made up of just one row of rings and chains. Made with size 8 white crochet cotton, it is about six inches in diameter.

Start at A on the diagram.
Ring A (3 – 3 + 3 – 3)
Turn
Chain (4 + 6 + 10)
Turn
Ring B (3 = 3 + 3 + 3) Join to ring A.
Turn
Chain (10 + 6 + 4)
Turn
Ring C (3 – 3 = 3 – 3) Join to ring B.
Turn
Chain (6 + 4)

Five-ring cluster
   Ring D (3 – 3 – 3 + 3)
   Ring E (3 = 3 – 3 – 3 + 3)
   Ring F (3 = 3 – 3 – 3 – – 1 – – – 1 – – 3 – 3 –
   3 + 3)
   Ring G (3 = 3 – 3 – 3 + 3)
   Ring H (3 = 3 – 3 – 3)
Turn
Chain (4 = 6)
Repeat around. There are six points.
Tie ends and work in.

Detail

Eight-Inch Doily

This doily looks like a snowflake made in white, or a flower garden made with flower-colored shuttle thread and mint or moss green ball thread.

Center is the small rosette (*page 13*).

Outside row is made like the lacy square (*page 21*), beginning with large ring A on the diagram.

Instead of the fourth point with a small ring, work **chain** (8 = 8). Join to center.
Repeat from A. The next small ring after that is joined to the previous small ring (see diagram).

24

Detail

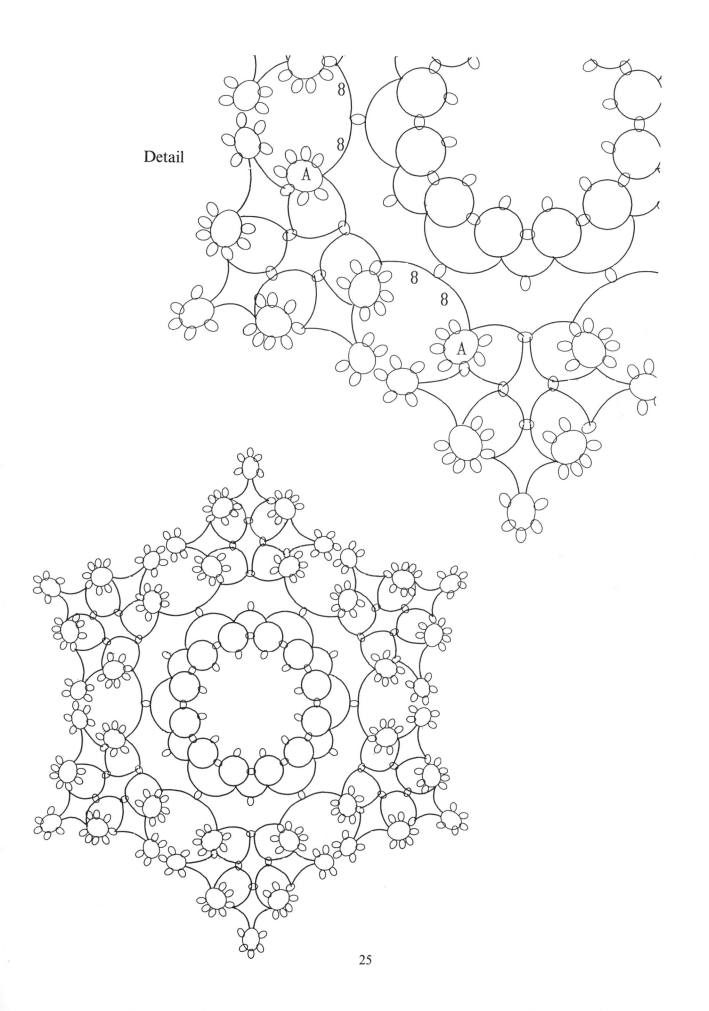

Tatted Necklace

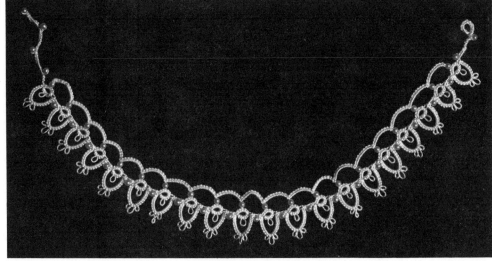

Materials: Crochet thread size 5 or 8 and about 45 small beads. Sample shows size 8 white crochet cotton with white beads.

The total length should be at least the neck measurement plus about three inches.

To make the necklace, string at least twenty-five beads on the crochet thread, then wind the thread onto the shuttle so that the beads are all between the ball of thread and the shuttle. Several extra beads may be used to insure that there are enough for the desired length.

Slide one bead so that it is held between the thumb and first finger of left hand. The first chain is made with this bead at the beginning.

Row one
Chain (bead, 8, bead, 8, bead, 8, bead, 8)
Turn
Ring (3 – – 3 + 3 – – 3) Close ring.
Turn
Chain (8 – 1 – – 1 – 8) Join to center picot of ring just made so that the ring is lying on its' side. Slide a bead next to this join.
Chain 1
Turn
Repeat rings and chains as shown in diagram until desired length is reached.

Chain (8, bead, 10)
Tie the ends around the last bead so that there is a loop large enough for a bead to fit through it. When two or three of the beads at the beginning of this necklace are pulled through the loop at the end, it will hold quite well and may be adjusted for a perfect fit. Jewelry clasps may be used to fasten the ends together for a safer hold.

Row two
Slide a bead onto the first picot of the first ring. Join the thread for row two to this picot. **Chain** 10. Slide a bead onto the next picot and join.
Repeat chains and beads so that row two is joined to all the rings in row one with a bead on each picot where joined. Diagram shows rows one and two together.
Tie ends and work in.

Because the exact length will depend upon the size thread used and how tight or loose the work is made, be certain to measure this piece. A choker should just fit around the neck. A long necklace would be made with more beads and to whatever length desired.

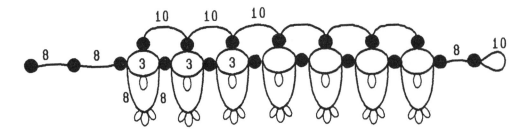

Oval Doily

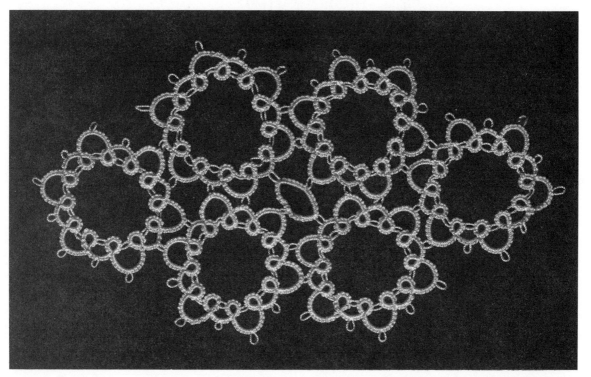

Make six small rosettes (*page 13*), joining them together as in diagram. The small chain of one rosette is joined to the large chain of the next.

When all six rosettes are in place, work an oval in the center. Join the ball thread to any of the four picots in the center of the doily, **chain** (7 = 7 = 7 = 7). Join to each free picot in center.

Tie ends to the first picot and work in.

This center chain oval may be omitted, however, it adds a nice finish to the piece.

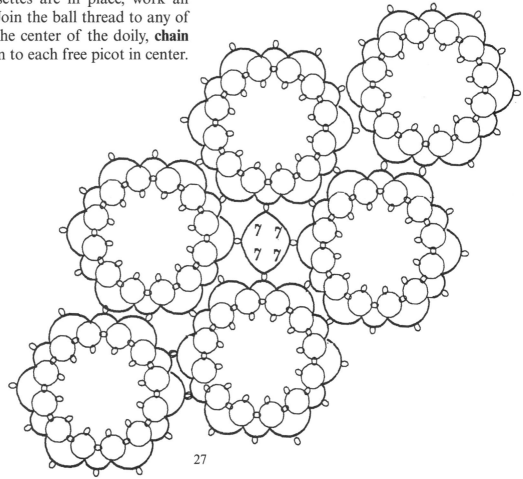

Lacy Table Mat

This mat is made from lacy squares (*page 21*) and circles-in-a-square (*page 21*) joined together. Actually the size and colors are changeable. Red shuttle thread and green ball thread make it resemble holly leaves and berries. The perfect item for that special holiday dinner table!

Lacy squares and circles-in-a-square are worked as shown in diagram. Make the lacy squares first. The example has the rings which join together as (3 = 3). However, it is easier to make them all the same as the lacy square. This project can be made as large as desired.

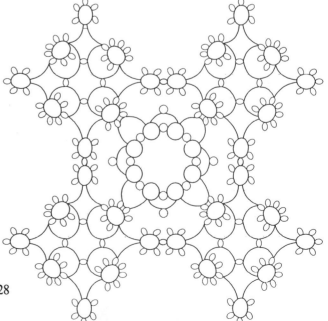

28

Flying Disc Doily

Approximately nine inches in diameter made with size 8 crochet cotton.

Center (*Fig. 1*)
   Ring (4 – 4 – 4 – 4 – 4 – 4) Tie ends together to form sixth picot.

First row (*Fig. 2*)
   Ring (3 + 3 = 3 + 3)
   Turn

Chain (4 – 4)
Ring (3 = 3 – 3 + 3)
Turn
Chain (4 – 4)
Repeat around, joining all rings together, and joining center picot of every *other* ring to picot of center ring.

Fig. 1.

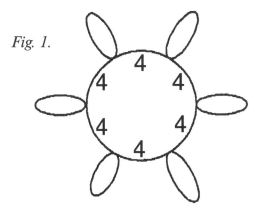

Fig. 2.

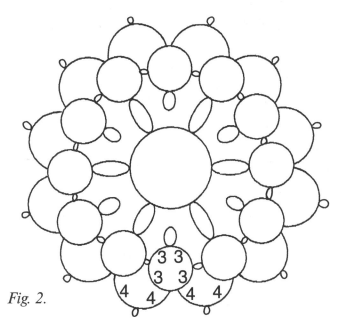

29

Second row—Sweet and Sour Rings (*Fig. 3*)

Small ring (3 − 3 = 3 + 3) Join to chain picot of first row.
Turn
Small chain (4 − 4 − 4)
Turn
Large ring (6 = 6 = 6 − 6) Join to previous ring and to next chain picot of first row.
Large chain (4 − 4 − 4 − 4)
Turn

Repeat around five more times. Every ring is joined to a chain picot of the first row. Each pair of small and large rings are joined together.

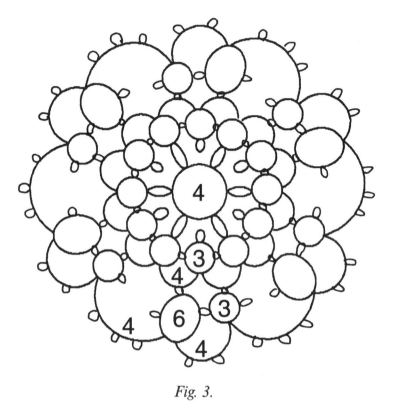

Fig. 3.

In order to make rows three and four easier to follow, they are presented in numbered steps.

Third row (*Fig. 4*)

Shuttle thread only. This row uses a lot of shuttle thread. When the shuttle is empty fill it and begin with the next ring. After completing the ring, tie the threads together close to the bottom of either ring. Cut off excess thread, leaving about six inches of thread ends. These will be worked into the piece when it is finished.

1. **Large ring** (6 + 6 + 6 + 6)
2. **Clover**
   Ring (3 − 3 − 3 + 3)
   Ring (3 = 5 − 2 − 5 + 3) Join to third picot of first ring of clover.
   Ring (3 = 3 + 3 + 3) Join to fourth picot of second ring of clover.
   Turn, leave ¼" space
3. **Large ring** (6 = 6 + 6) Join to second picot of first large ring.
   Turn, leave ¼" space.
4. **Clover**
   Ring (3 = 3 = 3 + 3) Join to picots of third ring of previous clover.
   Ring (3 = 5 − 2 − 5 + 3) Join to third picot of first ring of clover.
   Ring (3 = 3 + 3 + 3) Join to fourth picot of second ring of clover.
   Turn, leave ¼" space
5. **Large ring** (6 + 6 − 6) Join to second picot of second large ring.
   Turn, leave ¼" space.

30

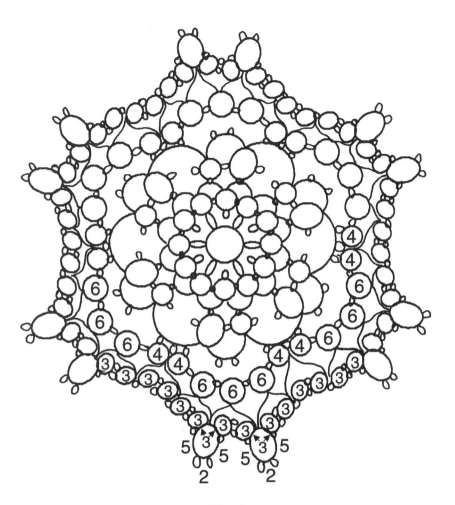

Fig. 4.

6. **Small ring** (3 = 3 = 3 + 3) Join to picots of third ring of clover.
   Small ring (3 = 3 + 3 + 3) Join to third picot of previous ring.
   Turn, leave ¼" space

7. **Medium ring** (4 = 4 = 4 = 4) Join to second picot of previous large ring and to two picots of large chain in second row.
   Medium Ring (4 = 4 = 4 + 4) Join together with picot of previous ring joined to second row and to third picot of large chain of second row.
   Turn, leave ¼" space

8. **Small ring** (3 = 3 = 3 + 3) Join to second and third picots of previous small ring.
   Small ring (3 = 3 + 3 + 3) Join to third picot of last small ring.
   Turn, leave ¼" space

Repeat steps 1–8 five more times

It is easy to make errors on this row, so join each clover and ring carefully. If you must stop for awhile, be sure to note where you are in the instructions. If you find you are making many mistakes, perhaps it would be better to work on this project when you are less tired or stressed.

Almost finished! Only one more row to go

Fourth row—Scallop border with more clovers and rings (*Fig. 5*)

Begin at A.

1. **Clover**

   Ring (3 – 3 – 3 + 3)

   Ring (3 = 5 = 2 = 5 + 3) Join to third picot of first ring of clover and to large ring (B) of third row.

   Ring (3 = 3 + 3 – 3) Join to fourth picot of second ring of clover.

   Turn

2. **Small scallop chain** (3 – 2 – 2 – 2 – 2 + 3)
   Turn

3. **Ring** (4 = 4 – 4) Join to middle picot of third ring of clover.
   Turn

4. **Small scallop chain** (3 = 2 – 2 – 2 – 2 + 3) Join to last picot of previous small scallop chain.
   Turn

5. **Clover**

   Ring (3 – 3 = 3 + 3) Join to second picot of last ring.

   Ring (3 = 5 = 2 = 5 – 3) Join to third picot of first ring of clover and to next large ring of third row.

   Ring (3 = 3 + 3) Join to fourth picot of second ring of clover.

   Turn

6. **Large scallop chain** (3 = 2 – 2 – 2 –2 – 2 – 2 + 3) Join to last picot of previous small scallop chain.

7. **Small ring** (3 = 3 = 3 + 3) Join to picots of third chain of clover.

   Small ring (3 = 3 + 3 + 3) Join to last small ring.

   Turn

8. **Repeat large scallop chain**. Join to last picot of previous large scallop chain.

9. **Small ring** (3 = 3 = 3 + 3) Join to picots of previous small ring

   Small ring (3 = 3 – 3 + 3) Join to last small ring.

   Turn

10. **Repeat** steps 8 and 9 three more times, then repeat step 8 once more.

Repeat steps 1 through 10 five more times. Join the last small ring to the first ring of the first clover. Tie ends and work in.

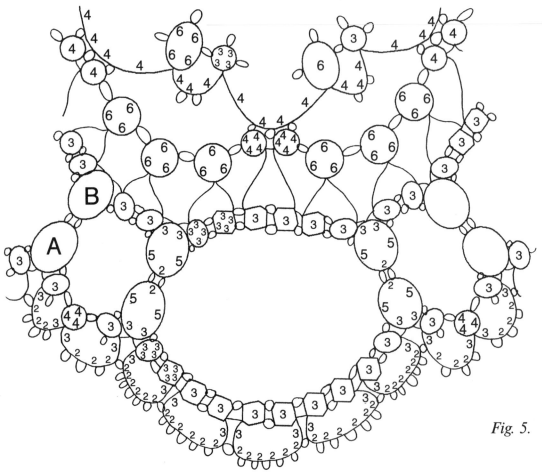

Fig. 5.